BURNED AT THE ROOTS

Enoch the Poet

Cover art by Oluwafemi

Black Minds Publishing is a national publications platform centered around the personal and professional growth of artists and creatives of the Black diaspora. At Black Minds Publishing we aim to give more visibility to raw artistic works, both literary and visual, that center on the healing process of the Black mind, body and spirit. We aren't concerned with the rigid expectations of academia or the "supposed to's" of artistic gatekeepers and instead choose to prioritize genuine works that have meaningful impact for its readers.

Names: The Poet, Enoch, author.

Title: Burned at the Roots

Description: Philadelphia, PA: Black Minds Publishing [2020]

Identifiers: 978-1-7356122-0-1

Table of Contents

Supplantation

My mother was given the name Tykisha,
the root of which, Kisha, means "rainfall."

                    My father and I share the same name, James,
                         which is Hebrew for "supplanter" or
                    someone who replaces by force or strategy.

I was born two days after my great grandfather's funeral.
I was born while mourning rainfall was still heavy on my family's
face.

              I was born a face on my great grandfather's shadow.
                              I was born a shadow.

                    A replacement.

                    A supplanter.

My great grandfather's name was Winston,
which has no specific meaning, meaning its
definition was my great grandfather.

       I was born supplanting a name only defined by the one who held it.

My great grandfather's middle and last name is James Church.
Church being defined as a sanctuary for worship.
If transformed into a sentence, my great grandfather
was a sanctuary defined by the things he chose to replace.

Read the bible to my great grandmother's
father every day because he couldn't read.

                         Became his gospel by replacement,

became his sanctuary by supplantation.

My mother never knew her real father
so my great grandfather became my grandfather

became her father by replacement,

became her sanctuary by supplantation.

He died then I was born and some family
think he became me by replacement.
Called me Winston and so I became
him by replacement.

My birth name is James.
My middle and last name is Winston Church.
If transformed into a sentence, I am a sanctuary
that replaces all the absence my family is defined by:

My aunt Sissie dies and the next day is my birthday.

My grandmother dies and the next week I graduate college.

My great grandmother dies and two months later it's my birthday again.

I was born to a rainfall and a supplanter
and I've been supplanting every rainfall since
I'm even a water sign.   A cancer.
And my great grandfather died of cancer

and I know those two things seem unrelated but
when I learned that my name means one who
replaces I couldn't help but feel like his tumor was
tied to my fate because how can a replacement

be born without anything to replace?

I was born an epitaph.

I was born a memory.

I was born and given a name that melded
my past and future together in one body.

I was born both root and branch.

I was born a _____.

Fractal

I am my great grandmother's son,
which means, I know well how to pick the weapons that form against me,
or in other words, I know what it is to be beat with a switch,
I know well the kind of lacerations that love can create,
or in other words I'm familiar with the love that grief demands,

which means, a great grandson can never be a replacement for a husband,
or in other words, Granny never mastered alchemy,
no matter how tightly she held me she still felt a void,
she knew I was one of her favorites but might not have known all the
reasons why,

which means, no matter what I did she was lonely,
or in other words, no matter what she did she was lonely.

either/or

mrs. delores from across the street hate me yo,
say i'm one of them "bad seeds," say i'm "no good,"
seen me run three niggas out my granny house one day
and i been a thug since. she ain't know i was throwing
hands for my sister cuz' mrs. delores don't ask no questions,
she just watch… and assume. if you ask her, she a
"good christian" so she always judging.

if you ask me, she just mad her son
answered the siren call of the streets and
now she need another ghostchild to chastise.

ms. chris though… ms. chris think i'm a saint.
she always throw a smile my way and i always throw one back.
shared a porch with me my whole life, seen me take
care of my great grandma like i birthed her, used to shovel her
snow in the winter and she'd cook us up some cornish hen for the hard
work.
if you ask her, I'm one of the nicest children on the block

if you ask me, she don't know enough about performance.
i am a nigga, which also means, i am an actor.
i play whatever role is needed for my survival.

they both right about me.

my niggas know best.
seen me bust a lip and make a simple syrup of the spill.
seen me crushed tender from the weight of life.
seen me smile too, and deep laugh, the kind that have
my great grandfather spirit bursting out my throat,
the kind my granny love cuz' it make her
feel like her baby still here.

what I'm saying is

even the hardest niggas fragile in the center.
even the softest niggas got jagged edges to cut with.

It's Dark and My Flesh is Hot
A Golden Shovel after DMX

I be a rude muthafucka', I be arrogant humble, I be a "I told y'all!"
ass nigga. I be a notebook cemetery, a ghost writer, as in, I been
writing out my ghosts for the past 13 years. I been eatin'
away at myself for sustenance. I be cannibal. Long
toothed vampire that can only drink its own blood. I be enough
but don't always see it. I be a continuous breakdown, I know
all the ways to die inside a poem because I can't stop
living outside of one. I be my own death dealer. I be in
and out of love with self but still want love from everyone. I be greedy.
I be manic sometimes, I be depressed sometimes, I be bi-polar, just
want to be happy but I've grown so comfortable with my sadness. I keep
a finger on the trigger in every poem. I be fed up with the bullshit.
I be tired. I be looking for the real but the real be real
elusive. I be Atlas to every partner
but still hear I don't give
enough. I be broke back to
hold up everyone weight plus my own. I be absinthe;
lover's drink me for a momentary fantasy. I be needy
but don't be needing nothing. I give up my ribs
to keep another nigga heart protected. I be searching for self in this
poem. I be masturbating in this poem, meaning, I be touchin'
the parts of myself that only I know how to love properly or moreso
that only I cared to learn how to love properly. I don't
be wanting shit from nobody. I be a Thanos remake.
I be noble villain, I got good intentions but don't nobody understand me.
I be impatient but always expect the wait.
I be a middle finger because I rarely give a fuck.
I be around but never actually around,
I be "gone boy." I be Hati and
Skol. I be sun and moon swallower, I'm
one heartbreak away from becoming Fenrir. Who gon'
be the Odin I sink my teeth into? I take a bite

of trauma and Ragnarok pours out my mouth. You,
as watcher, become empty vase and
I fill you up with all my sorrow. You snatch
a line out my breaking and make a compliment with it. The
plate becomes both full and empty. Eat off the plate. Clean the plate.

The Butterfly Effect

When I was in high school, my great grandmother began
referring to me by other family members' names.
A few years later I became a whole family within myself,
one day I'm her grandson, the next week I'm her brother,
the next month I'm her cousin or her uncle depending on the hour,

the next year   I'm   no   one.

The next year, she talks about my aunt's funeral but places
the face of my living mother in her casket.

My great grandmother begins to see half the family as both
                                                alive and dead

and she doesn't know the difference.

She becomes both   alive and dead

and she doesn't know the difference.

I imagine, somewhere in another time, maybe 1931
My great grandmother is playing in a house; her mother
calls her by a name that's not hers and it creates a ripple
effect that wipes her from herself 80 years later.

I call this anomaly   "The Butterfly Effect".

One small memory flapping in one time period
creates a ripple that grows big enough to erase
a whole great grandson in another.

Memories fluttering inside a great grandmother who can't remember
her name most days. A great grandmother who remembers the act

of forgetting but not what she forgot.

I imagine, somewhere in another time, maybe 1980
My great grandmother sits by her dying mother's side
but she doesn't have enough strength to say I love you one more time
and it creates a ripple effect that wipes my great grandmother
from this world in June of 2016. Laying in a hospice bed,
she says I love you to everyone in the room
but doesn't have enough strength to make it to me

        …I wonder what kind of ripple that will create.

Fractal

I am my Aunt's son.
which means, I make
some of the best pasta
on the east coast.

I boil, I spice, I blend.
I drawl out shiiiiiiittttttt
in front of elders cuz
somehow the drag makes
it not a cuss word.

I tender.

I don't always say
I love you first but
you can see it in my actions.

I spoil.

Both the kind that gives
too much to those who
desire and the kind that
holds me far past expiration.

I am ghost or
I do ghost or
I hold onto all
the loss until draining
it involves becoming transparent.

Until the only thing visible is
my voice, until I am a personality
in a bed and all you can see are

the sheets cascading over me.

When a Fractal Doesn't Know

My doctor says I have the flattest
feet he's ever seen, told me I could water ski on them
if I wanted to which I took to mean, I had no business
running indoor track. But I did anyway:

The soles of my feet crash against the cement floor
and a shockwave solidifies itself in
my lower legs.

I keep running though.

Learn how to quiet pain in strides.

Keep running.

Repeat 300s.

Keep running.

Repeat 150s.

Keep running.

Repeat doctor appointments.

Keep running.

I have love for my team, I have love
for a woman. In both situations
I run until I start to cremate
from the inside out.

Keep running.

Decomposition is a means of
communicating love.

Keep running.

A humming pain in my
foot spider-webs into
crackling knees.

Keep running.

Tender flesh turns
into swollen stone.

Keep running.

Nerves inflame between
bone and I gargoyle
from the knees down.

Keep running.

This is my first lesson in
how trauma can spread
through the body.

Keep running.

My doctor tells me if I
keep this up I can cause
permanent damage. My lover
tells me if I keep this up I can
cause permanent damage.

I keep running though.

Saturation

I wake up with a burning in my palms.
I've been sober for 2 months but still
start most days feeling a bottle in my hand,
still feel Jameson coating my throat.

I've been sober for 2 months but still
taste coconut rum in my spit,
still got Jameson coating my throat.
I swallow to get drunk off myself,

taste coconut rum in my spit
but ain't no real alcohol there.
I swallow to get drunk off myself.
I go to sleep nauseous

but ain't no real alcohol there.
I cold sweat Wild Turkey.
I go to sleep in parts.
My body a mixed drink.

I cold sweat Wild Turkey.
Drank so much wine it's in my blood.
My body a mixed drink.
I sip ginger ale and taste vodka.

Guzzled so much wine it is my blood,
drank myself into Christhood.
I sip ginger ale and taste vodka.
I think back to my last time

drinking myself into Christhood,
how easy it is to crucify oneself.
I think back to my last time

turning my throat into my grandfather's throat,

how easy it is to crucify oneself,
to take on all the sins of my family tree,
turn my throat into my grandfather's throat.
I become ugly and on fire simultaneously

to take on all the sins of my family tree,
a trunk of lit matches soaked in dark liquor.
I become ugly and on fire simultaneously.
I pray to the vices of fathers before me,

Henny soaked roots and a body of lit matches.
I hear God bouncing off an empty bottle,
I hear the whispers of fathers before me
and I think they both saying the same thing.

I hear God bouncing off an empty bottle
or maybe all this shit borrowed time and the bottle is God
and I think both statements saying the same thing
or maybe I'm the bottle and I been drinking myself to fill this vessel

or maybe all this shit borrowed time and the bottle is God
and that's why this phantom pain is in my kidneys like I'm still drinking
'cuz I'm the bottle and I was drinking myself to fill this vessel.
I've been sober for the past two months but still…

What Tenderness Can Cost Us

You work as a private duty
nurse in Cape Charles for four years.
You spend 8 hours a day caring for the

white people who hate you but a white man
gave you that job so you don't hate them back.
When not at work you give free check-ups to Black

families in the neighborhood. You
don't know it yet but duty is a slow death.
You spend Monday through Thursday

alone with the family while your husband works
a railroad job 300 miles away.
You wait for him to come home every weekend.

You don't know it yet but you are lonely.
Your feet ache and your joints are stiff
but you make dinner with the full of you.

You kiss him as soon as he walks in the door
and your lips chill as they brush against his gold teeth casings.
He lifts you as you hug and you remember his promise

to marry you back in the 8th grade.
Back then you thought it was bullshit but now its as
real as the God you pray to every night.

You work as a private duty nurse for four years
in Cape Charles until your family moves to Wilmington.
You don't nurse anymore so you make sure all

your daughters are nurses.

You nurse the entire family.
You nurse your husband when the cancer closes in,

the same way you nursed your mother years before him.
You see death but you never complain about
death. You just keep nursing more generations.

You nurse everyone you can, except yourself.

The Butterfly Effect

What if dreams were a glimpse into the multiverse? What if all of us were linked to all the other us's? What if last night when Granny appeared in my dream she wasn't a fabrication of my imagination? What if I was seeing her through the eyes of the other me? The me of that universe, another creation from another God with the same energy as my God and a different sense of irony. What if dying was just a transference of energy from you to another you? What if every death brought you closer to your complete self? What if, when Granny died, it wasn't a passing but a strengthening? Since 2016 she's been in over half of my dreams and maybe this isn't about the pain of losing or divinity trying to send me a message, maybe this is about all the versions of her resonating stronger at their points in time. Maybe this isn't a God thing and it's a ripple effect thing. I watched her splinter when Alzheimer's struck, become a grouping of personalities that all belonged to her but were no longer in conversation and now I'm here thinking what if this was spiritual feedback? What if multiple Granny's died before her in different universes at the same time and my Granny couldn't handle the transference? What if she fractured from the pressure? What if her mood swings were a congregation of energies increasing the gravity in her? What if, in those last years of her life, I'd been arguing with the wrong Granny? What if all the resentment I held should've been directed at an anomaly? How do you argue with an anomaly? My mother was re-diagnosed with cancer, worked a full-time job and still managed to bathe Granny, feed Granny, change Granny and in return I witnessed what it was to transmute a tongue into a pronged whip. "Thank you" into chastisement. Stress into a growing tumor. I witnessed what tenderness can cost us. I witnessed a mom withered by love. Who do I blame for these transactions? Who is accountable for the actions of a mind divided? Which Granny was really in hospice? Which Granny apologized? Which Granny whispered "I love you" into the ether loud enough for my mother to hear it and keep providing? Which Granny did she become when her body stilled? When the sickness ran its course, which Granny did her energy go to?

Fractal

I am
my uncle's
son. I know
how to drink
myself a new
identity. I know
how to keep a glass
of shape-shift gripped
tightly. Me and my whiskey Wonder
Twins, my mouth, a ring, this bottle
neck, a ring. I am my uncle's son so I
know aggression. I know the dermal
ringing of a closed fist. I know how
the impact ripples through the surface.
I know how friction can appease a broken
spirit. I know how to put a hole in some
shit. This is why I hate when people call
me aggressive because it sounds like calling
me my uncle and I don't want to be either
of those things. I am my uncle's son. I know
how to turn my depression into inspiration
for everyone except myself. I know solitude
intimately. I know darkness intimately. I know
the darkness of solitude intimately. I know
the weight of expectation. I know the fatigue
of not folding. I know the violences against
me and how easy they are to recreate.

When a Fractal Knows
After Dave G. and Christopher "KP" Brown

i was raised in a house
where the trauma of loving
a man was always more visible than the joy.

my grandmother praised all the men in my family cuz' she could only see
the parts my grandfather left behind. my mother praised no men in my
family cuz' she could only see the parts my grandfather took with him.
and my aunt praised me cuz' in her mind i was the closest she could get
to him.

which always made me think if a good man can leave all
this weight then imagine what a trash one can do. i never had
to imagine cuz' almost all the niggas in my family trash.

one uncle, lived around the corner the entire time we dealt with
grandma's Alzheimers and i ain't see that nigga until her funeral. one
uncle had so many run-ins with the belt that he became one, a lashing out
at everything he touched. one uncle loves his children with a clenched
fist. one uncle is a clenched fist.

the women in my family have carried men to the tops of Zion
just to have them forget who they God is. they religious but only
pray to themselves. they say a woman is only as good as the man
standing in front of her. they say real men should be fucking by fifteen.

they worried more about my dick than me but are quick to throw
out a homosexual slur and can't see the irony in that. the men in my
family live for the gaze of other men that never seem to

look in their direction. they only know the emotion of love
when it's tied to absence and so they only show the emotion of

love by making it absent. my mother's brother says he loves her but
i remember a time when "i love you" looked like him and her
husband forcing alcohol down her throat.

i say i love my sister but i remember a time when "i love you" looked
like me sitting silently when Dayday punched her to stop her from
crying.
i grew up around a bunch of men raisined with a lust for validation
and as a child i found myself shriveling in the same way: a desert fractal.

dried out and exhausted from all the absence around me,
this will not be a poem where the turn is a list of all the ways
in which i've changed because i'm still changing. still learning
how to be a person and still unlearning how to be a man.

Saturation

The scent of whiskey saturates my mouth with nostalgia.
My lips tense with memory and my fingers wrinkle with
an absent wetness. When I stopped drinking I realized
how easy it is to envy, at every gathering I thirst to be in
another's body. In these moments I am most demon-like,
trying to get drunk by practicing possession:

      my niggas sip a mixed drink and my tongue dampens
                    my niggas   take a shot   and my chest
burns
             my niggas   party foul   and my mouth
      widens   for   the scraps.

Fractal

I am my mother's son,
        which means I know
                what it is to be restrained,
                        to shackle oneself for
                                someone else's freedom.
                                      I know what it is to overflow;
                                          to bubble over. I know what
                                              it is to love with fear
and without it. I know what it
        is to take on feelings that
                are not my own, to empathize

myself into blindness. I
know what it is to lose control,
        control of a situation, control
                of myself, control of things I
                        never controlled in the first
                                place. I know not having control
                                      in the first place. I know how
                                      to perform joy, how to
smother a wildfire, how to blanket one
        paycheck across a month of

uncertainty. I know how to keep
        my problems cozy but most of all,
                I know openness. I know overcoming,
                        I know falling up and rising down,
                            I know how to use my spine for
                                  more than just my body, I know

lifting weight and the freedom that comes
        with letting that weight go.

What Tenderness Can Cost Us
From the perspective of my mother's back (After Julian Randall)

tell me child, have you ever carried a family? no, i mean
really carried a family? had the weight of each relative
grind your spinal cartilage into dust, to love a family, the
way we are taught, is to herniate, to allow your nerves to
flatten under the jelly substance oozing out the center.
you must become a vault of cracked vertebrae on

the verge of shattering into vacancy for the sake of
family posture, must have men hold peace in you
and still demand your curvature bend to their will,
privilege is funny in that way, how it gives a little to
take almost everything else.

i have bowed down on all fours for dogs who didn't
have the decency to lick the wounds they left
on me, been dragged raw against rigid house walls,
stood upright and bruised, loving through purpling
skin, i've had armies of fists explode against my surface,
examine it and you can still see fissures fathered along my spine.

i am swollen smooth, a mural of indentations
masquerading as love marks, and that's not to say
no one has ever loved me, just rarely ever more than
they have loved themselves, this is what it is to be
the soil that nourishes the entire forest.

every tree, young and old, roots in me, feeds off
me and gives barely anything in return, at night,
i sink wet into my mattress, let the foam dampen
to my contour, pray for a morning when i wake
up weightless, a morning when i rise and
carry only myself.

The Human Body is the Perfect Soil to Plant Love in...

After an image taken by Naji R. Copeland

A lover runs her hands through my beard and flowers bloom from the curls. A kiss planted firmly on the forehead grows an eden along my corpus callosum. We tangle under bed sheets and fruit grows in the folds where our bodies connect. An apple tree branches from interlocked fingers and a body turns into a forest and a heart turns into a seed and a body becomes richer soil and the process repeats and we think it's all pink backdrops and smiles until the seasons change and a branch falls and the apple tree splits in half from the shockwave of two hands pulling apart like split atoms and the bed turns to weeds 'cuz the fruits ain't getting watered no more and a phantom kiss cracks a forehead open and now two sides of the brain ain't thinking together and logic and emotion ain't agreeing and art sounding like a

dying flower now and a old lover runs her hands through my beard and her fingers come out cut 'cuz almost all roses grow thorns to protect their beauty but thats kind of ironic 'cuz the protection takes away from the appeal or something like that and this is all kind of ironic honestly 'cuz I started this poem talking about how the body is the perfect soil to grow love in and now I'm talking about all the ways my body can't

nurture a seed and it don't sound too hopeful in delivery but my family comes from a long lineage of people who learned how to grow from any soil. When I was young, my great grandmother would take me outback every weekend to help tend her garden. We would dig a hole in the dirt no deeper than begging palms and drop a group of seeds in. She would say "you need affection to grow a flower" so we would take our fingers and massage the seeds into the land, bury them inside the begging palms and baptize them in water. Our backyard started out a graveyard and my great grandmother turned it into a greenhouse, taught me how to love the soil enough

to grow a garden.

Supplantation

Raw.　　　　Black. Raw Black.　　Lustful.　　　　Curved spine and
soft skinned.　　Hard shelled Cancer.　Bald headed Medusa. Stared at my
reflection so long I stoned myself.　　Dry eyed bastard child of north side
Wilmington.　　　　　Griot of the broken home.　　Thug with a pen.
　　　Black Uchiha. Last of my lineage.　　　　Masochist.
Recovering.　　Bourbon bodied.　　　Fire throated.　Scorch skinned West
African descendant.　　Planted.　　　Country watered in a city garden.
　　　Raised on cornmeal pancakes and scrapple.　Raised on cloudy
water and 40 ounces and Jesus Christ and crack rocks and NY Fried
Chicken on Market street and Pete's Pizza and E-Z Mart where I used to
steal hot pickles and A.I. Middle where Du punched a girl in the face for
taking his seat in social studies, where Mr. Martin wore dress shoes with
no socks and shot the fair one with Jaron 'cuz he got tired of the ashy
ankle jokes.　　Where the cops was called, a few times.　　Where Eric
thought I was weak 'cuz I let niggas clown me and he found out the hard
way my hands was faster than my comebacks.　　Where most niggas
thought I was angry but at that age anger is usually just emotions we ain't
been taught to process, 'cuz our parents weren't taught to process and
their parents weren't either and how could they be.　I come from a
household where silence was tradition. Where you don't have a teary eye
unless you in front of a casket.　　Where a boy much older than me
killed a piece of me three rooms down from Auntie's room and I ain't go
back to that house until her funeral almost 20 years later.　And it was
still silent there.　　And I was still silent there.　But I've gotten
better with speaking now and I've gotten better with anger now and I see
emotions and I name them and I make space for myself and some of my
friends see me for me and some of my friends don't and I make peace
with that.　In my own way.　　　I make peace.　And I'm
doing better, and I'm doing better, and I'm doing better and I'm paying
attention to who loves me the right ways and spending less time
complaining about who don't and I say "we" when I talk to my niggas
about anything 'cuz if one of us go through it then we all do, that's how
family work and when I say family I mean the ones I chose.　　Life

is all about choosing.   and listening. and listening before you
choose.   and unconditioning.   and freedom. It's mostly about
freedom.

The freedoms you give
the freedoms you get
and the freedoms you take back
because they were always yours to begin with.

Acknowledgements:

First and foremost, the people I will always thank because of their role in my personal and poetic development and the amount of love they pour into me consistently and unconditionally (some of y'all will get mentioned twice lol): my amazing, supportive and loving partner: Jasmine Hawkins; my poetry niggas: Kirwyn Sutherland, Kai Davis, Jasmine L. Combs, Christopher KP Brown, Lindo Jones, Marquis Wright-Lee; my brothers in growth: Daniel Woodley, Ronald Daughtry, Antoine Tucker, Anthony Tucker and Jesse Johnson; my sister: Zaria Brown; my father: James Clayton and his wife Carolyn for providing me with a place of refuge while I worked diligently on this book; my mom: Tykisha Church-Brown, for hours of conversation about family history and helping me connect the dots that led to the creation of some of the poems in this book.

I also want to thank the homie Femi for introducing me to the concept of fractals and unknowingly giving me the missing link to my book and also for creating an amazing book cover.

Yolanda Wisher for hours of council/wisdom and taking the time to talk with me about generational trauma.

Julian Randall for the impromptu conversations about poetry theory and inspiring the poem "What Tenderness Can Cost Us," as well as Kassidi Jones for pushing me to experiment more with poetic forms.

The Philly Pigeon for hosting/funding the poetry retreat to Vermont that helped get me over the hump when I reached a wall with finishing this book.

Breedlove and the Freedom Party for providing a safe space for me to try out new work and process through my writing by way of performance.

The fellow poet homie Dave G. for all the heart to hearts and conversations around healthy masculinity and its relationship to tenderness and for playing a role in inspiring the poem "When A Fractal Knows."

All the poets I study tirelessly because of how inspiring I find their works and lives to be: Porscha O., Rasheed Copeland, Thiahera Nurse, Franny Choi, and Jamaal May.

I would also like to mention Yolanda Wisher, Rasheed Copeland, and Kirwyn Sutherland again for agreeing to be editors for my book and assisting me in making it the complete project it is today.

I would also like to give thanks to the following publications for giving some of the poems in this book a home before the manuscript was complete:

- **Wusgood POC Magazine and Apiary X** for publishing "The Butterfly Effect"
- **Noble Gas Qtrly** for publishing "The Human Body is the Perfect Soil to Plant Love In"
- **Open Minds Quarterly** for publishing "Its Dark and My Flesh is Hot" and "Supplantation #2" (titled "Saturation" in this book).

And finally, I want to thank the matriarchs of my family: My great grandmother (Mattie L. Church), my grandmother (Lena Dorenda Barron), my aunts (Willie Mae Pettijon, Anne Green, and Mattie Strong), and my mother (Tykisha N. Church-Brown) who taught me tenderness, resilience and all their nuances.

If there is anyone I forgot just know that it isn't because you weren't important or because you didn't play a meaningful role in my life, it's really because my memory is shaky and I'm writing these acknowledgments on some last minute shit. Love y'all and I hope this book was everything you wanted it to be and more.

About the Author

"Those days, I used to ask him what he feared, and he always said, 'the bottom of a good glass.' And then he stopped answering. And then he stopped coming home altogether." This quote from Hanif-Willis Abdurraqib's book, *The Crown Ain't Worth Much (2016)*, speaks to the condition of Black people and how our struggle to survive can dissolve us into absence. It is also a testament to Enoch's purpose as a poet, to bring those who fear the bottom of the glass back home.

Enoch the Poet was born and raised on the north side of Wilmington, DE. He is a an author whose work examines the process of healing and the ways that trauma and mental health move through a family, as well as the outside forces that affect or have affected these developments. His goal is to create work for the younger him, work that deepens our emotional understanding and its cyclical relation to the conditions acting on the Black mind, body, and spirit. In 2017, he won the title of 2017 Philadelphia Fuze Grand Slam Champion and placed 28th out of 95 in the Individual World Poetry Slam in Spokane, Washington.

Enoch's had work published in various literary magazines such as Wusgood and Open Mind Quarterly and before the end of 2017 he published his first full length book of poetry titled "The Guide to Drowning." Off stage Enoch is a teaching artist who creates curriculum that uses poetry as a medium for processing trans-generational trauma. When he's not performing or teaching you can catch him reading manga, watching anime or serving underprivileged communities as the Treasurer and Creative Director of Urgent 365, Inc, a non-profit working to move communities of color forward through resource distribution, education programming and social wellness events.

Enoch is also the founder of Black Minds Publishing, LLC, a national publications platform centered around the personal and professional growth of artists and creatives of the Black diaspora.